A COMPILATION
OF
THOUGHTS

Kurtis O. Graves II

Library of Congress Cataloging – in- Publication Data has been applied for.

Paperback ISBN: 979-8-9859916-8-0

PRINTED IN THE UNITED STATES OF AMERICA.

FIRST EDITION

I'm Here

Don't ever feel as if you must prove you exist.

You live, you breathe, you bleed,

The fact that you exist, validates you existence.

Stop fighting a battle that you've already won.

Realize that the world is already aware of your existence.

Table of Contents

Dedication

This book and all the rawness of life, struggle, pain, frustration, and hope expressed in it are dedicated to my son Nyiem Kurtis O'Neal Graves. I don't know, but I have an idea, of how difficult your life has been, and I need you to see that you are not alone in your struggles to exist, and learn who you are. We are on this journey together and forever will be. I hope that who I was, who I am, and who I ultimately become can always be an example to you of your ability to persevere and overcome any obstacle you face. When you read these words, I hope you feel supported. I hope you feel loved. I hope you feel wanted. And I hope you know and feel that you're not alone. Especially in your darkest times.

<u>Special Thanks</u>

I wanna give a special thanks to everybody who has made this project what it is and who have supported me through this journey called life one step at a time.

Special thanks to Ivory, the mother of my children, and the reason that my world continues to spin. The 1st person to read the words you're about to, and really see the person who wrote them for who they were. You not only read my thoughts you read me. You stepped in and filled a void that was so huge, that I almost disappeared into it. You gave my life the purpose that I needed to be here today, and you supported me when my life was so low that I felt like I was crawling. Every project I've pursued and every attempt to better myself you have been, and continue to be, the hands and feet that move me forward. You've given me a family and a purpose in many more ways than one, and I will forever love you and be grateful to you for it all.

Thank you to my Father and Mother Curtis and Ginger. Both of you have shown me since my birth that my survival and my life were always a priority to you both. You have supported me and carried me when the world left me for dead. I can never repay you for never giving up on me. And I will never stop trying as long as there is life in my body.

Thank you to my siblings Rayshonda, Rhonnell, Katrina, and Clayton. Y'all have been my starting 5 from day one, and I will forever be thankful for being born into your team. What connects us is deeper than blood, and I look forward to exploring and expounding the relationships that my incarceration had diminished and hindered.

Thank you to my Gram Olevia Singleton, my Grandmother Mary Graves, my Grandfather Wilbert Richardson, and my Grandfather Ernest Clayton Graves. You all are the foundation and bedrock for who I am, and for who our entire family is. Thank you for caring for and supporting me in y'all own special ways my entire life.

Thank you to my Aunties Patrice Warren, and Auntie Zelle (Jazelle Plummer). Y'all always made me feel loved wanted and special and I thank you for that.

Thank you to all my uncles. There's way too many of y'all to list, but to the standouts Uncle Steph, Uncle Cyd, and Uncle Fonzie. Thank you for giving me a foundation of being a man in each and every of your own ways. All of you have given a unique example of what a man is and should be, and I will forever value the contributions of who you are and the impacts you've made in my life that includes all eight of my father's brothers.

To my many nieces and nephews. Too many of y'all to list as well, but y'all all make the list. Y'all taught me how to love when my heart was ice cold. Y'all loving me and getting to know me from a prison cell, made me feel like I had something and someone to fight for. Y'all helped me become the Uncle & Father I value being above all else.

To my Bros. Kwame Lamar Walker, Jihad the General Jihad, Reggie Sanders, Lamar Rambert, David Bookman, Pierre Marcel, Dayron Malloy, Sire, Cole "Young exact", Loi Nghiem, Damien Phillips, Kyle Maddela, Bricks, Black Moe, Barry Moore, Randall Jones, Taji Lee, Heem, Zay Diddy (You already know bro!), Terrell "TJ" Graves, Zakaria Ajlane, Trigg, Lil Nard, Lee E. Colston, Lamont "Big Unc" Campfield, Martique Daughtry, Grant Paige, Rah Gundy, Gregory Womack, Nyree Abdullah, Uncle Ike, Wiz, Su, Stedie Dume and the many more I don't have the space to name. Thank you for the role you've all played in me becoming who I am and growing into this man that has stood tall through it all. Y'all contributed so much and rode with me against an endless ocean of Opps. We still exist because they can't do nothing with us and they know it. We got a lot more to do, and I'mma love y'all forever.

A special, special thanks to my bro Eddie Ray Gray.

Who stood with me for no logical reason when he didn't have to. You showed me that it was okay to show the world who and what I am. You put me on this path by walking down it 1st and showing me the way. I ain't gotta say much to you because you already know. KOBA!

To Benjamin Herold. I already told you, but I'll say it again the First Person Documentary you invited me to be a part of taught me how to process who I am. You made this book possible. Physically as well as foundationally. Thank you for being the solid and consistent friend and mentor that you are.

Great Grand mom. I miss you, and the opportunity that is lost for me to get to know who you are and all that you survived. Thank you for being the pillar and pivotal piece in my journey to becoming me.

To my In Laws Mama Lovy, Papa Phil, Uncle Drip, Rell, Aunt Sandy, Grandmom Rudine, Ebb, Anna, Kelley, Wayne Wayne, Jess with a J, Alicia, Nuri, Sasha, Stephanie, Sophia and all the many others (also too many to name) who went out of y'all way to accept me and welcome me as an extended part of your family. I thank you for the honor that you did me. And I hope that upon my release I can show you that I am indeed worthy of that honor.

Most importantly to my Lil People. Nyiem & Zaynah. Y'all are more important to me than either of you will ever comprehend. Y'all unleashed me, and allowed me to be what I was always meant to be, and what I've proven to be the very best at, and that is a father. Thank you for loving me, and wanting me in your lives. Thank you for choosing me. Thank you for believing in me. I have not even scratched the surface of expressing my love for either of you. I promise to give y'all this whole world and some. I'm almost there, and there I'll forever stay. Thank you for trusting me with your hearts. Thank you for trusting me to stay when others haven't. I love y'all forever and a day.

Author's Note

This work is a compilation of thoughts. Personal thoughts written down to emphasize the internal conversations I believe are necessary to better understand ourselves, by bringing to life our hidden feelings of frustration, pain, anger, despair, sadness and hatred. I believe that fully understanding the why behind our feelings is the only way to truly understand ourselves, as well as the people and the world around us. You may relate, or you may not. To the people who do, I feel for you and with you. Just make it to tomorrow.

A COMPILATION OF THOUGHTS

The Reminder of Pain

I trust pain
It's honest and constant

Pain allows me to feel
It gives me comfort

Sometimes it's the only proof I have,
that I'm still alive

I need pain,
it gives me strength

The more pain I suffer,
the more I know I can endure

Pain is a good thing,
it keeps me honest with myself

Because of pain,
I will never forget,
what people are capable of

Pain's Virtue

Pain is everywhere.

I feel it with every beat of my heart.

With each beat joy floats away,

    and pain floods my veins.

The pain of loss, the pain of gain.

The pain of mortality, the pain of time.

Anger, hate and a thirst for destruction.

The fire of life sputters,

    but I refuse to let it fail.

I will kill to live, I will die to be free.

I live in a purgatory, that feeds off the insanity,

    that simultaneously kills the body and soul.

Death is certain in the life of every man,

I have never feared it, because to me death is peace.

Death is the only true release of pain.

I look forward to that peace one day, the grand finale,

    to the story that is the life of me.

A Compilation of Thoughts

But as I live I breathe, with each breath my lungs fill
with the pain of life.

I continue living because the story of me is incomplete.

I don't flee pain, I embrace it.

I swim in the pain of life, I let it hydrate my soul.

I let it fortify and strengthen the essence of me.

My foundation is strength and pain,
and the strength of pain

I was born of anger, depression, loss, and betrayal.

My people lost their world and their lives,
their culture, beliefs and worth.

For centuries they struggled, they fought, bled and died.

They shaped their destinies,
to pave the destinies of their children.

They paved the destinies of my grandfather and his father,
my grandfather's sons.

My destiny has been paved with the pain of progress.

My pain enriches the world, my pain weakens the hate of
ignorance, and repairs the damage of indifference.

My pain is the sword I wield against failure.

Death is not to be feared, nor pain, nor sacrifice.

Kurtis O. Graves II

Fear is to be confronted, overcome, and dismissed.

To succeed you cannot fear to lose everything.

Who am I to whine, cry and complain?

Is my life more precious, than those I love?

Does life promise joy? Love? Or success?

No! Life promises Death!

Only the will to live, the will to succeed, the will to try,

    promises the fulfillment that we all desire.

L2D (Live to Destroy)

I live in a place of destruction.

All that resides here is destructive people,

doing destructive things.

I live in a destructive cycle, that can never destroy itself,

because destruction itself is an infinite cycle.

Where I live we destroy ourselves, the very air we breathe

seeks to cease the beat of our hearts.

The destruction of this place is not orderly, its chaotic.

For a time, you avoid the brunt of the destruction,

only to have that chaotic force destroy your false sense

of hope, of escaping its destructive nature.

A sad many people dive into destruction,

hoping to win an unwinnable battle,

by adding their power to an already unstoppable force.

Many end up in the ultimate place of destruction.

It's funny because once they get there, they tend to

give up like they had no idea this place existed.

Kurtis O. Graves II

If I ever end up in the ultimate place of destruction,

    I will throw back my head and laugh.

And destroy every one of them, who crosses my path.

Goodbye

I can't keep giving

Where's mine?

I'm hungry, I'm thirsty, I'm tired.

I'm sad, angry and frustrated.

I've been hanging off this cliff for lifetimes.

My fingers are getting tired.

I no longer have the strength to pull myself up.

If I let go and fall, no one will be there to catch me.

I no longer care.

I no longer wish to be caught.

I don't owe you anything.

I've done my part.

If I live or if I die, I'll learn the truth.

Kurtis O. Graves II

I'm letting go.

Because I refuse to continue to give you the satisfaction of

watching me struggle.

I see your fear, and now I smile.

You know that you've lost me, because my fear can

no longer keep me in place.

Where will I end up?

I don't know.

I only know that you cannot follow me.

You're too slow.

You have too much baggage.

And you're too afraid.

We will never be in the same place again.

I have no more questions for you,

And you won't receive any answers from me.

You're dead to me.

Goodbye

It's time for me to move on

A Compilation of Thoughts

Don't try reaching for me.

I don't want to be touched.

I hear you, but I'm no longer listening.

I see your eyes pleading and begging,

But it's too late.

You'll do better you say.

You'll try harder.

Even if I believed you I wouldn't hold on.

There's too much I need to do.

I can't do that holding on to you.

Q.T.L.

What do you care about? What do you think about yourself? Your future? Do you just float by, day by day? What matters to you? Who? Does anyone know you? What do you know? Do you know anyone? Who do you know will, without a doubt, always be who you know them to be? Who cares about you? Can you be trusted? Are you interested in religion? God? Or do you just want the truth? If I could prove to you that you can have everything, would you accept my proof? What I have to give? Or would you run, afraid that it "might" be a lie or trick? What are you afraid of? Why do you care? Do you have faith in you? What does it take to earn your trust? Who do you trust? What does it take for you to see the truth? If you were left alone, and surrounded by nothing, what would you say then? Would you cry? Yell? Drift away? Or would you make the world yours? How many burns does it take to prove fire is hot? Who runs from freedom into captivity? Why run from life into death? Why lay down and die beside an unlocked door, rather than take a chance at living with what's on the other side? Is your blind fear really more powerful than your will to live? What makes you think? What makes you refuse to? What makes you afraid to try? Why are you afraid to answer your own questions? What makes you who you are? When will you stop being afraid? When will you think about you? If you had a month to live, what would you do?

Circles

I run track.

I get on a track and run.

I could run for hours, days or weeks at a time.

When I stop running. I'll still be on that track.

I lose time, but gain what?

What are the benefits of chasing your tail?

Even if you catch it, What's next?

When I stare into the eyes of my past.

I see who I was, not who I wanna be.

So, what am I running for?

Who am I chasing after?

What am I running from?

A Tired Soul

Life is hard,
But living is easy

You only need to live for a moment
Find your moment, own your moment

Take a deep breath and smile
Pause life and live in your moment

Good pain, sad joy
No worries, no decisions

Delusions are allowed in your moment,
Because they can't exist in life

Life is pain, anger, more pain and stress
Life is victory, defeat, pain, and success

Kurtis O. Graves II

To participate in life, you need a strong will,

To live all you have to do is stop caring,

To die all you need to do is give up.

Giving up is never an option,

Fighting has always been a choice.

My Life

I don't need you, but I want you

Without you,

I honestly believe I'd be just fine

But with you,

I believe I can change the world

Without you,

Nothing I've done, up to this point, will mean a thing

But with you,

The things I do from this point on, can save so many

Without you,

My growth ends

But with you,

My potential is endless

You know who you are

I don't need you but with you,

We can do so much

You are...My Life

Kurtis O. Graves II

Why do I need vision,

When there's nothing to see

I'd rather watch the back of my eyelids

Than stare into this reality

The darker it is

The better I feel

Golden Rule?

Stop!

Stop what you're doing for a minute and close your eyes.

Imagine your life and everything in it.
Now do your best to imagine mine.

Imagine that we only have a little more time.

Now reverse our roles.
You living my life and me living yours.

Would I treat you the way you treat me?

Do unto others…

Authority's Flaw

Authority only goes so far.

If you tell me to "Stop" and I stop, you have authority.

If you tell me to 'Wait" and I wait, you have authority.

If you tell me to "Stay where you are!" and I advance to your position and plunge a knife into your throat, your authority has ended.

Remember that.

Tears

Sometimes I cry

I cry for the people I've lost

I cry for the people I'll never know

Sometimes I cry for the people with no faces

The people with no names

Resting in unmarked graves

Life should be priceless

But to most its worthless

My name is Kurtis O'neal Graves II

I sit here alone and cry for you

I cry for you, so sadly I have no tears

To cry for me

M.A.D.
(Mutually Assured Destruction)

If I stop caring about going home,

You won't be

A Thought

Anyone can have everything.

Sadly, no one wants anything.

Another Thought

You can never make every move available to you, but if you are aware of all your possible moves, you stand a much better chance of making the right one.

It's Time

In the space between forever and never, all you have is right now.

Heartless

I'm heartless

When your heart is broken into a million pieces,

You're bound to lose some

I lost so many, that I simply discarded the rest

I'm heartless, but I remember how it felt when I wasn't

I remember loving my heart,

Now I hate love

Love was my mistake,

Pain was my punishment,

Remembrance helps me suffer,

Destruction made me tougher,

Burying those pieces changed me.

Being heartless remade me

Queen

I met a tiny woman a long time ago.

She was only tiny until I saw her, then she began to grow.

Her personality swallowed everything,

    and her smile rearranged the cosmos.

The way she moved made the world burn,

    her eyes froze the flowing rivers.

She laughed and I cried tears of joy,

    a sound so beautiful, that no darkness could destroy.

Physically she was light years away,

    but her presence I felt in an instant.

The warmth of her touch reduced me to ashes,

    while the energy of her breath reinvigorated my soul.

She collected every bit of me,

    even the pieces I didn't know were mine.

She reconstructed me and loved me until I ran out of time.

She taught me to think and succeed,

    then sent me on my way.

Kurtis O. Graves II

She blessed me with a kiss,

    and a promise to reunite, someday.

I searched for her, yet she was gone.

Teaching me more with her absence.

From lifetimes away she held me,

    keeping me from going backwards.

That tiny woman was a giant, as she is to this day.

If my tomorrow never comes,

    I know she'll love me anyway.

I will destroy my world to protect her,

    making it safe for her to stay.

All her nightmares and dangers I'll cast away,

    each and every day.

She owns the world and everything in it.

The Ultimate, Dominant Being

Each day all life bows down to her.

All Hail the most Phenomenal Lovely Queen

Things Left Unsaid

It's sad, dark and quiet

I wanna smile, but smiling hurts

Laughter is the same as crying

And crying is non-existent

Only a few get to smile

Only a few get to laugh

Only a few get to love

Week Zero

Tomorrow it begins

I've come to the end of caring

The end of trying

Tomorrow I will start to hope

I have no faith,

None whatsoever

But tomorrow I will start hoping

Week Three

I've started something
Now I'm afraid to stop

If I stop hoping now
I feel like I'll lose

I've cursed myself
With something I didn't believe in

Now I believe that if I stop and I fail
It will be my fault

So, I'll continue hoping
For as long as I can

Week Six

In most instances, words aren't as important as deeds

But in a lot of cases, the right words can evoke

    spectacular actions

Words without deeds are often useless

As are deeds without the proper words to explain them

I find it hard to find the words,

    that accurately explain why I am who I am,

    and why I do what I do

Someone told me to continue being true to me

So, I've realized that even if you don't understand me,

    I do, so that's explanation enough

    for me

Week Eleven

Purpose

It's a word that holds more meaning than it is accredited

It is a word full of power

It's not something you can create

You serve it without realizing

Because it's something you can't control

A puzzle's pieces all align because they're supposed to

Your purpose helps the world fulfill its purpose

To every question

There is always an answer

Even if it's not your purpose

To know it

Week Thirteen

I have a simple question

When you're completely and utterly alone

Does anyone really care?

Week Fifteen

I used to think boundaries were put in place to contain me

I was wrong

Boundaries help you define what is and what isn't

They show you, your weaknesses and reveal your faults

Boundaries allow you to be you

They protect you

They guide you

Without boundaries, I'd spread myself so thin that

    I'd disappear

Boundaries are put in place to keep you together and

    to always remind you who you are

Week Eighteen

Today I'm fine

Free to hope, free to care

Free to try

Free of insecurities, doubt and fear

I won't claim to understand everything

But there's one thing I know

My Heart Smiled

My heart smiled today

There's always something to make you smile

Even when you feel like you're dying

A joke you were told, maybe one you've over heard

Even a personal one that you didn't understand

Until the point when it no longer mattered

But the things that can make your heart smile are much rarer

A certain person

Or a dream you wish you never had to awaken from

When your heart smiles, you hold onto that for as long as you can

Today my heart smiled

That's all that matters today

Week Twenty-Six

Who I am...

I'm intelligent and strong

I'm creative and positive

I am more than I appear

Who I can be...

I can be cold and calculating

I can be vindictive and a tyrant

I can destroy many people and things

Who I'm going to be...

I'm going to be who I am,

The opposite of who I can be

And much more than I can imagine

Week Thirty-Four

I've never made a million dollars

I've never been around the world

I've never changed history

Nor do I envy anyone who has done these things

I have done something equally great

Something few truly ever do

I've used everything I've learned, to stop being a child

And became a man

Week Fifty-One

Thank you for changing me

Loving you saved me from never knowing love

Thank you for letting me love

Loving you showed me how to love me.

A Clearer View

I once asked, why do I need vision,

  when there's nothing to see?

I once stated, I'd rather look at the back of my eyelids,

  than stare into this reality.

Nowadays I hate closing my eyes,

  because I know there's always something to see.

Even in the darkness.

Kurtis O. Graves II

I was born of victory, so I'll never know defeat

A Black King met a Black Queen,

who made a Black Prince

That prince became a King who met his Black Queen

That King survived the stresses and turmoil

that plague, black royalty.

That King strived, stayed alive,

and gave birth to his prince

That prince struggled, that prince fought

By recalling all he learned and was taught

Through strength of will, that prince became this King

This King defeated defeat

This King is victory

Victory is me.

Black Is...

Black is a solid color. It's not loud and flashy, yet it still remains defiant and strong. Black is capable of quietly and humbly making a powerful statement. Black is relatable. It can complement any other color without being drowned out or dominated. Black is confident. It exists in many forms, in every culture. Black is everywhere, and silently refuses to disappear. Black is victorious with or without competition. Black is the absence of all color. Color depends on light to be seen, but black is independent of such necessities. Black is the foundation. It is the absence of the lies that we tell ourselves. Black is freedom from unjust expectations and damaging trends. Black frees you from seeing what everyone else is doing, so you can focus on yourself. Black is an example. Black exists, and thrives, whether the world chooses to acknowledge it or not. This is why Black is my favorite color.

Kurtis O. Graves II

Some people lay down to sleep hoping that tomorrow
    will be better than yesterday.
I on the other hand know that tomorrow
    will be better than yesterday
If you wake up to a tomorrow,
    you can reminisce and enjoy
    the memories of yesterday
While preparing, planning, and making more memories
    of today
But if you do not wake up to a tomorrow,
    your yesterday will cease to exist,
    along with your today
Thus, meaning yesterday has no value unless you can
    compare it to today
And you won't realize how good today is
Unless you wake up tomorrow

Choosing Forever

The space between forever and never is its own measure
of eternity

You can immortalize yourself right now or die forgotten

Right now, you have every opportunity to succeed, even
though it seems that failure is inevitable.

If you surrender, you die.

If you box yourself in, you perish.

Conformity is destruction.

Salvation only exists in freedom.

Freedom only exists in Choice

Choice is the only constant Truth

The truth shows me, ME.

And the truth of me sets ME Free.

Kurtis O. Graves II

A Beautiful Dream

Two small round dots

Bright and Brown.

Reflecting the world

Without making a sound.

A row of white

Top and bottom

Easing your worries

Erasing your problems

I looked into her round face

And the world slowed down a while

I never realized the power

Of a daughter's smile

Longing

A smile is a powerful, beautiful thing

It can change your day from horrible to wonderful

Can simultaneously fill you with both joy and pain

It can set your loins afire

The joy comes from the pleasure of being in the presence
of its radiance

The pain of having such beauty in your presence yet not
being able to obtain it

You long for your smile to meet theirs

Yet, there is such pain in knowing, that it never will

Tomorrow's Promise

Today is the last day I will see any of you as you are today.

Tomorrow the you of today will have withered away

Does that frighten or sadden you?

I wonder why it is that we cling on to our pasts.

Why is it so important for us to quit?

With blessings waiting around the corner,

    why do we stay on the block?

Who determines what risks are worth taking,

    and which are not?

What is the truth, and why do we hate it?

What matters? And what can we ignore?

I trusted in a lie prior to meeting you today.

A vicious lie of anger and hate.

I built a reputation of ugly pain,

    and painted murals of suffering.

Like many of you I stopped caring,

    before I ever learned how to.

A Compilation of Thoughts

But today I thank God that I'm blessed.

Yesterday I turned that corner

    and walked into the blessings of today.

The truth that I used to hate is the truth that sets me free.

Without Him, there is no me.

I've never been enthusiastic

    about admitting my weaknesses.

But I've come to realize my greatest weakness

    is my strength.

I've come to understand that there are things

    I simply can't do.

And that made me realize there is nothing He can't do.

And also, the things I can't do

    are extremely possible thru HIM

I pray that today each and every one of you

    walks away from yesterday

I trust that you will trust the truth and hate the lies

I hope that you don't quit on your future

    by staying stuck in your past

If your ultimate destination is heaven,

    why do you believe that He would lead you

to stand on the block for eternity?

What matters more?

Yesterday or Tomorrow?

Are you willing to ignore all that tomorrow might bring

to die today?

Don't let your future wither away.

Destroy those murals and discard that reputation

Overcome your fear and sadness,

and say goodbye to the you as you are today.

I love you all and I'm going to miss you dearly

But I pray that tomorrow you'll look in the mirror

and see today more clearly.

Just a Wish

Happy Birthday

Everybody dies. Some people die young, some die old. Most people spend so much time worrying about what people think of them in life that they forget to live. When I die, I wanna remember your smile. No frowns, no tears. When I die, I wanna know what love feels like. As I die, I wanna feel love so I can remember life.

Leaving

I won't forget.

I won't forget any of you, not even for a second.

I refuse to leave you here to perish.

I refuse to forget any of this.

I will not face the world incomplete,

> by leaving a chunk of who I am, behind.

I can't leave that chunk because I need it,

> so it must come with me,

> because I can't come back for it.

I won't.

I am who I am, because of the Truth.

And the Truth is, I am who I am.

You don't get that do you?

I do. Maybe someone else will too!

I smile because there's no fear, no shame, and no regret.

I'm not dragging behind any baggage.

A Compilation of Thoughts

I'm clothed in my many layers of blessings.

Who I am has never been a secret.

If you listen, I'll tell you.

You can come with me, but I can't drag you

You have to know who you are, in order to travel

How do you find out who you are, you ask? Simple

Listen closely because I'm leaving after this,

    so you'll have to remember

Purpose, Control, Patience, Faith, Love and Understanding

There's someone who knows exactly who you are and

    why you're here

Ask him. If you listen, he'll tell you.

Hurry Up! I'll see you outside.

Amante

The inspiration you give is also my torture.

You hold the keys to my existence, yet you free me in pieces.

The most painful anxiety is standing at the threshold of your desires, and not being able to partake.

As you draw nearer, it becomes harder to breathe.

Because your breath becomes mine.

If you refuse to share, I will slowly but surely die.

20-40 Years Away

I learned to fight long ago

I'm glad I did, because I need to fight

I fight for survival and success

It's a very long fight

In long fights, power and speed lose relevance

It boils down to control

I want to master control of myself

So that I can win this fight

Losing this fight means I lose everything

I care about way too much to lose!

The Last Choice

I am going to die.

I am going to die one day.

What will I leave behind?

If I died tonight, what memories would I leave behind?

The people who remain and remember me,

    what will they remember?

What is more important?

The things I will take with me,

    or the things I'll leave behind?

Reality

When does better come?

Hope is toxic

As destructive and deadly to a heart and will as a bullet

  to the brain

Continuing to care is begging to be continued by pain

Damage now comes from every direction

I am assaulted on my right and left

Mercilessly stalked from my enemies from behind,

While starring into the face of an instructible army of hole

Where is my solace?

How far away is my peace?

Where are my allies?

If I am meant to fight this war alone,

  should I just change my enemy and perish valiantly?

"When" I perish, will it matter "how" I perished?

Will my valor be recognized?

Will it be relevant?

Kurtis O. Graves II

Will the cause of my demise be known to the people I love?

Will they know that I lost a battle

to an overwhelming, undefeated foe?

Or will they believe that I surrendered,

defeated by my own cowardice?

Is there a differentiation between how one meets his fate?

Who will ever wonder how hard I fought?

How many enemies I overcame?

Who will contemplate my undying will to succeed,

to live that perished along with me,

even as I fought and failed?

If it is one thing that I could/would say to the world,

it would be this...

"...I never gave up. I never surrendered.

I fought with all I had, but I lost."

Perfect Perceptions of a Disaster

There's a fine line between perfection and disaster.
Perfection exists in your perception.
While disaster is a creation of your perception,
of everyone else's perception.

If the sky is beautiful to you,
then love the sky.

If rain feels good upon your skin,
then love the rain.

If everyone around you thinks the sky is too bright,
or that the rain is gloomy.

Does it become a necessity to deny the perfection of your
perception, of the beauty that surrounds you?

Perfection exists in your perception.
If you perceive yourself to be beautiful, you are.

Expand your perception.
Allow yourself to perceive your perfection.

The Power of Me

I walked through the night
And shook off the darkness
The anger that chained me
Fell away as I changed

I walked up to that mountain,
I misled, then I moved it
I looked back and felt a weight upon me
I faced forward, took a step, and felt free

Danger is the destination of anger
Why fall victim to you, when I can conquer myself?
You can never hope to own me,
Because you've never known me

Why are you in such a rush to slay me?
Do you hate the fact that I no longer fear you?
Or do you fear the fact that I now know what I can do?
I do love the fact that you're consistent
What makes you the angriest with me is this powerful
truth…
I am no longer angry with you.

A Good Question

Why do we seek comfort in conformity?

Why do we trade in our individuality for a false solidarity with strangers?

Why do we fear being unaccepted as we are?

Why do we convince ourselves that what we are isn't enough?

When do we start to question what we've known as the truth since our first breath?

Why do we question who we are but quickly accept, without doubt, the person people want us to be?

If we conform, why do we not conform to our own standards of beauty and perfection?

Why do we avoid our creativity?

What do we need to do to enjoy who we are, as God intended?

When do we intend to start?

A Dream Deferred (For My Mother)

There's a saying,

If you want to make God laugh, tell him what you have planned.

A solid saying that I will not use as an excuse.

Even though your plans did not match HIS plans, they still matter to me.

You never closed your eyes and imagined, with joy in your heart, your son sitting in a cage of my own making.

When your eyes closed, and your mind's eye opened…

You saw me smiling and heard me laughing.
You felt my love through the power of my existence.
The strength of me imposing my will upon this world.

Your heart circled the world twice in a moment, propelled by the elation of your deeper vision.

Kurtis O. Graves II

Sights of me being a proper father, brother, son, husband, and man.

A dream deferred.
I say deferred because it still exists.
The vision you saw is still there to see.

Close your eyes and imagine me.
Your child, your pride, hope and joy.
Your son!

See me be the man I am. The man you've raised me to be.
See me reach the heights invisible even to your mind's eye.
Watch me climb higher than any plan or dream you've ever imagined.

In every person's life, they will always know disappointment. Your disappointment at your dream deferred is not ignored. In fact, it is the motivator of this man of your heart.

I had to disappoint you. I'm sorry!

But if I didn't, how could I surprise you with who I am right now?
If I didn't, how could I get you to understand that our previous plans were too small?

A Compilation of Thoughts

If I never disappointed you, how could I make you proud?

I need you to understand that in order to give us a bigger dream and clearer vision, I had to destroy our expectations!

I trust you! I trust you to care for me as you always have.

I see you, and you see me, but what is missing?

Close your eyes and remember your old vision, your dream deferred. What has changed?

Us! We have changed!

You want more for me now than you ever wanted for me then.

Why?

Because you know I am more than I was. I can obtain more, and I deserve more.

We deserve more!

I know your disappointment. I know your dream deferred.

Kurtis O. Graves II

Trust me!
Trust me to be the son you've raised.
The man you've watched grow.

Kill your disappointment and renew your faith in your dream. Better yet, dream the better dream. The dream in which your disappointments are just the joke that made HIM laugh.

I am disappointed that we believed that we had to settle for a dream that now seems so very small.

T.A.I.M.
(The Animal in Me)

There's something inside of me that reminds me of you.

Something that refuses to break, bow, or surrender.

When I close my eyes I can see it,
And when it's quiet, I can hear it.

It lies just below the surface.
It slumbers, yet stays alert.

If you look deep into my eyes, you'll see it staring out,
seeing everything that I don't.

I glimpsed it in your eyes when I was a child, but I didn't
understand.

I didn't understand what lurked behind the smiles, and
beneath the manners.

I didn't understand what was hidden by the suits and
uniforms.

Kurtis O. Graves II

The character of a man can only be revealed once he's seen life.

Not the delusions of youth, but Life!

That something inside is awakened when it's time to say "Enough"!

When you must say "No!" to surrender! When you must continue to fight even when everyone else believes the cause is lost.

That something is always relaxed yet, poised to attack. Fear, anxiety, frustration and anger feeds it, along with desire, ambition and pride.

When I think of you, that something inside of me growls. Pride and a call of blood makes it rise.

I have inherited your source of strength, and your unconquerable spirit.

We are undefeatable, because that something inside of us, converts every set back into a victory.

Finding My Way

At one time, I lost.
I lost the ability to see, feel, or understand.
I didn't know up from down or left from right.
I didn't know what was good, bad, right or wrong.
I cared, but I didn't know how or about what.
Nothing was wrong, nothing was right.
Nothing mattered.
Simple things were complicated.
And complicated things were impossible.
Everything that mattered was pointless.
Everyone that mattered was gone.
All that was left was me.
When I was alone, I realized I was there.
When I realized I was there, I realized I mattered.
Once I realized I mattered, I was happy I was there.
When I lost, I won.
I miss you a lot, more than is possible.
I lost you. I lost me.
I found myself, my way, and my reason.
So now I'm winning for us!

A Close Friend

I took one step, then another.
I stopped to rest, and got lost.

I took one step, then another.
I looked for you, and got lost.

I took one step, and then another.
Then another, and another.

I didn't look, but I felt you here.
You weren't in front of me,
> behind me,
> or on either side of me.

When I felt you closer than ever, I tried to grab you.
The minute I did, you were gone, and I was lost.
My frustration was foolish. It's obvious I thought.

I sat down and waited. I waited and waited and waited.
Nothing happened.

I stood up and took one step, then another.
You were right here.

Decision Time

I love you, but I hate who you used to be
You used to be naïve, ignorant, selfish, and petty.
You were wide eyed with wonder,
    at all the things unwonderful.

You were weak, ill mannered, simple,
    and just plain stupid.
You were irritating and extremely wasteful.
You thought you had all the answers,
    yet you didn't know shit.
When I think about who you used to be,
    it makes me sick.

When I think about who you could've been,
    it makes me smile.
When I think about who you will be, it makes me proud.
You had a lot of good qualities,
    but they were masked by the ill ones above.
You changed your life in good and bad ways,
    you eliminated self- hate and learned to love.

Kurtis O. Graves II

You love like no other,
    because you see the error of your past ways.
You now make decisions guided by love,
    not anger, hate, or rage.
You are a rare individual,
    very special indeed.
Some thought you couldn't change,
    you've made a believer of me.

I love who you are, what you stand for, and why you care.
I understand who you used to be
I'm glad that you've grown and I'm glad that you're here
I am you, you are me.
Let the truth be laid bare.

Ambition's Crossroad

There's so much anger inside me, yet it is justified

I rage against stagnation.

I thirst to destroy any and all ideas and forces,

That despise progression.

My indignance and aggression remains pure,
    because it is simple

I hate cowardice.

I hate the critics who hate themselves and their people.

They are quick to judge and slow to act.

Their flaw is their cowardice.

They fear to evolve
They fear to grow

They ignore the pains of life,
    seeking instead the mercy of oblivion.

Kurtis O. Graves II

Failure is a deceit.
One man can change the world, one person at a time.
One man just has to be willing to try.

Some men are willing but unable.
I am willing, but I am trapped.

There is a curse of injustice to a man who cares
  but is incapable of showing it.

Each has his chance.

So be angry with yourself.

Only you can choose to pursue the deceit of failure,
  and not the world.

Oblivion

So much joy, revealed by false smiles
So much happiness, expressed without laughter
So much love, received with no heart
So much pleasure, never felt

Such an evil amount of good
Such a destructive force of hope
Such a beautiful sight of despair
Such an incredible taste of defeat

Oh, how I hate the smell of cowardice, how I am so
thoroughly embarrassed, by the lies I hear that fools are so
quick to absorb as truth

I see the world through the eyes of a Man, a Savage, a
Citizen, a Heathen, and a Saint. I see the world through
the eyes of the Weak and the Strong.

I see the world through the eyes of the blind, those
blissfully born that way and those who consciously
choose, each moment, to remain unconscious. I care not
for excuses, only the truth.

Tiring Relationships

She walked slowly at first, but as I grew closer she disappeared around the corner

So, it is my assumption that she quickened her pace

I rushed to the corner to try and catch a glimpse of her, but when I looked she was not there

I looked behind me and saw her walking away from me in the opposite direction

I ran after her and her pace increased, and though I was running, I knew I'd never catch her, so I stopped

When I stopped, her pace slowed

I sat down on a stoop, and she seemed closer

As I sat, I watched as she continued to slowly move away

I feel tired, frustrated, and irritated

Increasingly irritated with myself for my lack of motivation

I feel that I should be doing something, but I can't

Because there's nothing I can do

I close my eyes and take a steadying breath

A Compilation of Thoughts

When I open them, she's there staring into my eyes like she's waiting for something

I make room for her on the stoop

She sits

Tired and exhausted, she smiles at me

I smile back, and we rest

The Truth

There is a natural beauty to the truth. An allure that entices fools to pursue their own destruction like a moth to a flame.

Truth is a vision. A perspective and perception. The truth is hollow, yet its roots are deep. The most beautiful thing about truth is its conviction. The conviction that is not diminished, nor dismissible, by the fickleness of the true nature of truth.

Beauty is a speculation. Truth truly lies in the eyes of the beholder. We can both agree that the sky is blue, or we can take the world and tear it in two.

My truth is as real to me, as empty is to oblivion. The truth of life lives in your smile, and in the twinkle of your knowing eye.

I pursue the truth in the dreams of my heart. When I wake I look back at the distance I've traveled, and marvel at the pain that has paved my steps.

Forward is the abyss that stretches eternally. The partner

of truth who jealously protects her beauty from the foolish and undeserving.

Harnessing the warmth of truth, is the same as maintaining the fires that burn in oblivion. The power to perceive the truth, is the freedom to pursue destruction, yet I still prefer no lies.

I live and survive on a precipice of hope. Balanced between my equal desires to live and die. Balanced on a peak as the winds of truth's demands howl around me.

Many truths exist, born from each breath. Truths that both succeed and perish in their moment of conception.

I look upon you with longing and desire. You belong to me, yet you exist in a world that my breath does not reach.

The Truth, is that my future does not exist. The truth is that no future exist except the future that is an elaborate lie.

Understanding truth births potential. Yet the truth is that all things true are also potentially false.

Nothing lasts forever. Nobody is eternal. Truths?

Kurtis O. Graves II

Nothing lasts forever. Nobody is eternal. Lies?

The only truth that matters to me, is the truth of your existence. The only way to truly love, is to truly love the whole.

You exist as a whole. Your Truths and Your Lies are the perfection of your completion.

Yesterday I met you. Today I've loved you and tomorrow I am already at peace in the enveloping, cascading honor of your presence.

Every promise is a potential lie, yet who tells you more lies than your own heart?

The truth is a beauty, that lies to your face. That's why I accept the truths that lie beneath your lies.

To deny a part of you is to love none of you.

You are the biggest part of me. I am the abyss that embraces you.

The Disconnect

In my world, everything makes sense
Trees always grow
Birds always sing
The only thing that dies in my world is me

I perish and I'm reborn,
time and time again

In my world I fear nothing,
except that our time can end

In my world I struggle,
but as I struggle I grow

In my world you laugh and sing,
struggles you never know

In my world there are no words,
because we know how each other feel

My world is perfect for you,
Sadly isn't real

Kurtis O. Graves II

In my world you're happy,
Because I'm never mean

My world exist in my mind,
So, it's just a dream

Alone

It's so quiet, that my thoughts are screaming
Everyone's staring at me but no one sees me

My mother sees her child
My sister sees her brother
My nieces see their uncle
But no one sees me

I see her
She's no one
Yet she's everyone

She has everything and I have nothing
I want everything she has, but she wants nothing

I'd give everything I have for her to see me
And all I have is my life

She doesn't want to see me,
Because she has everything
And I am nothing

I just wish that no one could see me

Thoughts of Costs and Loss in February 2022

And for all the relationships that didn't last up to here.

That moment we had.

That window of opportunity.

The intense, world consuming, powerful phenomenon of endless possibilities, that is the make or break point of any and every relationship.

That minute spectrum of relative time, so improbable, that finding it the first time was in every way illogical.

That special privilege bestowed divinely, never to be taken lightly, was simply dismissed…?!

I'd be lying to myself in disgust if I failed to discuss the depths of my truest feelings towards you.

I hope that every single moment your image is reflected, that you look upon it and stew.

I pray for however many gods that may hear it, that the moment you lost ME haunts you.

Excerpt from
Forthcoming Collection of Shorts

I know what's important. Everyone's lives always have a crossroad. Some have many. At each crossroad a choice must be made. You must choose which direction to travel. Some decisions will be easy, some less so. Whatever your choice your only true option afterwards is to live with your decision.

September of 2002. High school. Everybody who has attended high school remembers high school. Some memories are fond, some filled with anger or pain. Mine? I ain't even gonna lie, I love my high school memories. I had fun. I really started to come into my own there. Here now starting over, I have those memories, but I'm not looking forward to reliving them. My beliefs and understandings now will corrupt those memories. My knowledge has corrupted my interactions. So, in essence, my memories have corrupted my memories. I can't experience life in the care free manner of children. I can't experience the joy of life, without it's pain. But this experience is an important part of the story, so I'll share every bit of it.

Kurtis O. Graves II

Riding the 48 bus, public transportation has always been fun for me. It felt right. I've always enjoyed people watching. I was once those rowdy kids in the back. Watching them now I suppress a smile. Who has the energy to be a complete asshole at 7 in the morning? Loud and boisterous. Every action screaming for attention but feigning indifference to the people around. It is just human nature, all of nature. It is a natural desire of all things to be allowed to be. To be allowed to exist as one sees fit. Yet most of us ignore this instinct in favor of conforming to the wishes of those above us, of those around us. I move my eyes over my fellow occupants of this bus. Starting at the driver. Who as a child aspires to be a bus driver? To deal with hundreds of different demeanors daily. Some aggressive, many obnoxious, a few even down right hateful. But is the bus driver perturbed? No. the driver comes to work each day and drives. The driver is no fool to delude themselves that today will be a perfect day. That today no one will seek to anger, threaten, cheat or harm them. Nor do they show up to work anticipating today being any amount more difficult than the day before. Life is as it always was, whatever you make it to be. This bus driver was probably like me as a child, a rowdy, aggressive, troublemaker, and only thought of himself. Eventually though the driver realized that there is much more to life than attention.

A Compilation of Thoughts

Have you ever noticed that the driver is usually the quietest person on the bus? They are content and free. Content to be honest and free. A man can respect a bus driver's choice of destiny, even if he seeks not to mirror it. I as a man can respect another man, who is sound of mind enough to make a choice.

About the Author

Kurtis Graves was born in North Philadelphia and lived there until his incarceration 26 days after his 16th birthday. At the time of this writing he's been incarcerated 17 years and 3 months with still a road to travel. His greatest passion is family and he does everything in his power to daily build himself into a surefooted and consistent asset to those he loves & cares for, without letting his environment and circumstances determine who he is allowed to be in their lives. He fights daily for his freedom and the blessing of supporting and investing in those he loves uninhibitedly.

Kurtis is also the founder of the growing online movement The Survivors Community. Visit the website @ www.thesurvivorscommunity.com.

www.ingramcontent.com/pod-product-compliance
Lightning Source LLC
Chambersburg PA
CBHW060333130626
46553CB00003B/1006